APR 2016

SPECTACULAR
SPACE SCIENCE

Exploring the
SUN

Nancy Dickmann

rosen publishing's
rosen
central

New York

Published in 2016 by The Rosen Publishing Group, Inc.
29 East 21st Street
New York, NY 10010

First Edition

Produced for Rosen by Calcium
Editors for Calcium: Sarah Eason and Jennifer Sanderson
Designer: Greg Tucker
Consultant: David Hawksett

Photo credits: Cover © Dreamstime/Laurence Romaric; p. 5 © Shutterstock/Jose Ignacio Soto; p. 6 © Shutterstock/Juan G. Aunion; p. 7 © Shutterstock/a40757; p. 8 © Shutterstock/Iryna1; p. 9 © Dreamstime Kenneth/Sponsler; p. 10 © Dreamstime/Anthony Baggett; p. 11 © Dreamstime/Charon; p. 12 courtesy of NASA/SDO/HMI; p. 13 courtesy of NASA; p. 14 © Shutterstock/EMprize; p. 15 © Shutterstock/Balazs Kovacs Images; p. 16 courtesy of NASA/SDO/GSFC; p. 17 courtesy of Hinode/JAXA/NASA/PPARC; p. 18 © Shutterstock/Designua; p. 19 courtesy of Wikimedia Commons/Mike Garrett; p. 20 © Shutterstock/Elena Korn; p. 21 courtesy of Hinode/JAXA/NASA; p. 23 © Shutterstock/Dmitry Kosterev; p. 24 courtesy of NASA/H. Zell; p. 25 © Dreamstime/Zina Seletskaya; p. 26 courtesy of Skylab, NASA; p. 27 top courtesy of ESA/NASA/SOHO; p. 27 bottom courtesy of NASA/SDO; p. 28 courtesy of NASA, ESA, J. Hester (ASU); p. 29 courtesy of NASA/JPL-Caltech; p. 30 courtesy of NASA/JPL-Caltech/STScI/CXC/SAO; p. 31 © Shutterstock/Jens Beste; p. 33 © Dreamstime/Olesiaru; p. 34 courtesy of Wikimedia Commons/JgFRcI7gLXKP2Q at Google Cultural Institute; p. 35 © Shutterstock/THEJAB; p. 36 © Shutterstock/Sue Stokes; p. 37 courtesy of Wikimedia Commons/kubotake; p. 38 courtesy of NASA; p. 39 courtesy of Wikimedia Commons/Arches National Park; p. 40 courtesy of JAXA/NASA/Lockheed Martin; p. 41 courtesy of NASA; p. 42 courtesy of NASA/Goddard Space Flight Center; p. 43 courtesy of NASA/SDO; p. 44 courtesy of NASA/Joel Kowsky; p. 45 courtesy of NASA/JHU/APL.

Library of Congress Cataloging-in-Publication Data

Dickmann, Nancy, author.
Exploring the sun/Nancy Dickmann.
    pages cm.—(Spectacular space science)
Includes bibliographical references and index.
ISBN 978-1-4994-3621-1 (library bound)—ISBN 978-1-4994-3623-5 (pbk.)—
ISBN 978-1-4994-3624-2 (6-pack)
1. Sun—Juvenile literature. I. Title.
QB521.5.D53 2016
523.7—dc23
                                                                    2014048785

Manufactured in the United States of America

CONTENTS

Chapter One

GOD OR STAR?

From the tiniest bacteria to the tallest trees, almost all life on Earth depends on the sun. Humans need its light to see, its heat to keep us warm, and its energy to support life. The sun is incredibly important to us, but it is not unique. It is just one of billions of similar, medium-sized stars found in our galaxy and elsewhere in the universe. However, for most of human history, people did not realize this. Instead, the sun was seen by many as a sort of god.

For the ancient Egyptians, the sun represented light, warmth, and growth, and was depicted by Ra, one of their most important gods. Ra was believed to have created all forms of life by calling their secret names. However, the sun god could be a destroyer as well as a creator. In one story he became angry with humans and sent his eye, in the form of the lion-headed goddess Sekhmet, to punish them.

The ancient Greeks saw the sun as a god called Helios, who drove the sun across the sky each day in a chariot pulled by flying horses. This was their way of explaining why the sun moves from east to west each day. Other cultures have similar myths serving the same purpose. For example, Norse myths tell of the horses Arvakr and Alsvid, who pull the sun's chariot.

In Hinduism, Surya is the sun god. His sons include the first man on Earth, the lord of death, a great warrior, and king of the monkeys. Surya had the power of banishing darkness and curing disease.

TEMPLES OF THE SUN?

Even thousands of years ago, people could accurately track the sun's position as it changed throughout the year, and many ancient structures were built to match the sun's position in the sky. For example, the stones at Stonehenge in England are aligned to frame the sun during the summer and winter solstices. The Mayan pyramid of El Castillo is designed so that serpent-shaped shadows appear to slither down its sides during the spring and fall equinoxes.

This temple at Chichen Itza, in Mexico, is just one of many ancient structures that were designed to align with the sun's position at various times of the year.

Ancient Astronomers

The sun was important in religion, but some ancient astronomers studied the sky in a more scientific way. For example, more than two thousand years ago, Babylonian astronomers were able to trace the path of the sun along the ecliptic over the course of a year. The ecliptic is an imaginary line in the sky that marks the annual path of the sun. The Babylonians were able to see that at some points the sun seemed to slow down or speed up, though they were not able to tell why.

A lot of astronomy depends on mathematical calculations, and the Greek mathematician Eratosthenes (c. 276–c. 194 BCE) made a number of discoveries. He was the first person to calculate the circumference of Earth, and his figure was fairly accurate. He may have calculated the distance from Earth to the sun, too. Not all scientists agree on the translation of his Greek writings, but one version is incredibly accurate. Hundreds of years later, the Greek astronomer Ptolemy (c. 100—c. 170 CE) estimated his own figure, which was way off.

Many historians believe that Eratosthenes invented this tool, called an armillary sphere. It is used to demonstrate the motion of stars around Earth.

Astrolabes were used by astronomers to track and predict the locations of the sun, moon, planets, and stars. They could also be used for navigation.

WHAT IS THE SUN?

The Greek thinker Anaxagoras (c. 500–c. 428 BCE) was determined to find out how the world worked. He believed that everything followed natural laws. He was the first to suggest that the moon reflects light from the sun, which is true. However, he was wrong about other things. He thought the sun was a mass of blazing metal the size of the Peloponnese, a large peninsula in Greece.

Between about 700 and 1500 CE, the Arabic world had its own great astronomers. They studied the stars, and many of them (such as Betelgeuse and Aldebaran) are still known by their Arabic names. They used tools such as astrolabes and armillary spheres to observe and measure the positions of the sun, planets, and stars. For example, the astronomer Ibn Yunus (c. 950–c. 1009 CE) recorded more than ten thousand entries of the sun's position over a period of many years. Other Arabian astronomers noticed that the points where the sun's orbit seems to slow down changed over time.

Putting the Sun at the Center

Although the sun was recognized in ancient times as being crucial for life on Earth, most people believed Earth was the center of everything. Earth stayed in one position, they thought, and everything else traveled in circles around it. The sun rose in the east and moved across the sky to set in the west, and ancient people believed that was because the sun was traveling around Earth, and not the other way around. It naturally followed, then, that everything else revolved around Earth, too.

Ptolemy figured out a model to show how the solar system worked. His version had the moon orbiting closest to Earth, followed by Mercury and Venus, then the sun. After that were the other known planets in the correct order. However, although on the surface this seemed to work, the mathematics of the theory did not quite match up with people's observations.

Copernicus was worried that his ideas would cause controversy, and he was right. His book was published just before he died, and it was banned for many years.

There was one possible solution for these problems: what if Earth and the other planets actually orbited the sun? A few ancient philosophers, such as Aristarchus of Samos (c. 310–c. 230 BCE), had proposed this, but they were not taken seriously. In the sixteenth century, the Polish astronomer Nicolaus Copernicus (1473–1543) published a book that took the world by storm. He brought together centuries of observations and calculations to figure out a model that seemed to match what people had observed. However, it took more than a century for his ideas to be widely accepted.

GETTING THE ORDER RIGHT

Although he was not the first to figure out the order of the planets, Ptolemy was right in saying that Venus and Mercury were closer to Earth than the sun was. Very rarely, Venus passes exactly between Earth and the sun and can be seen as a black dot moving across the face of the sun. This is called a transit, and the Persian thinker Avicenna (980–1037 CE) may have witnessed this as early as 1032. The transits prove that Venus is closer to Earth than the sun is.

A transit of Venus is a rare occurrence. The last one was in 2012, and the next will not be until 2117!

9

New Ideas

The telescope was invented at the beginning of the seventeenth century, and for the first time, astronomers could see phenomena such as mountains on the moon, the moons of Jupiter, and Saturn's rings. The telescope also helped reveal more about the sun. For example, astronomers were able to see sunspots more clearly. These had been seen before, but were usually thought to be objects transiting the sun. Galileo Galilei (1564–1642) studied them and realized that they must be on the surface of the sun.

In 1672, Jean-Dominique Cassini (1625–1712) calculated the distance to Mars. Based on this, he came up with an accurate figure for the distance to the sun. Many discoveries during this period had to do with analyzing the sun's light. For example, in about 1666, Isaac Newton (1642–1727) used a prism to show that the sun's light could be split into rays of different colors.

Isaac Newton was one of the greatest scientists ever. In addition to his work on light, his theories about gravity and physics helped astronomers understand the motion of the planets.

In 1800, William Herschel (1738–1822) took this a step further when he discovered infrared radiation. There are many types of electromagnetic radiation, and the light that we see is just one of them. Types of electromagnetic radiation are classified by their wavelength. Herschel was using colored filters on his telescope when he discovered that some colors made the telescope heat up more than others. He had discovered infrared light, which is invisible to the human eye.

In the nineteenth century, astronomers began to use spectroscopy to study light. All substances absorb light at particular wavelengths, and by studying the light that reflects from an object, scientists can learn what it is made of. Joseph von Fraunhofer (1787–1826) found lines in the spectrum of sunlight that corresponded with elements in its atmosphere.

When light is split by a prism, it always shows the same spectrum, consisting of red, orange, yellow, green, blue, indigo, and violet.

STUDYING SAFELY

It is incredibly dangerous to stare directly at the sun, especially through a telescope. Its light can permanently damage your eyes. Astronomers such as Galileo were able to study the sun by looking at it at sunrise or sunset, when its light is not as dangerous. Many of them also used their telescopes to project the sun's image onto a white card, which they could look at safely.

Chapter Two

A LOOK INSIDE THE SUN

The Earth and the other planets are spheres, but they are not just simple lumps of rock or balls of gas. Each planet has its own internal structure, with a central core and various different layers. The sun is no different. Over the years, astronomers have been able to identify several different layers within the sun.

No one has even seen below Earth's crust, but scientists are fairly sure that beneath it is a mantle of dense rock that can behave like a fluid, then a liquid metal outer core surrounding a solid iron inner core. Scientists can figure out this structure by studying the way that seismic waves from earthquakes travel through Earth. In the same way, we cannot see inside the sun, so astronomers must use the available clues to figure out what is inside it.

Although the sun is not solid, the photosphere (where sunspots appear) is often referred to as its surface. Inside it, the gas is so dense that we cannot see through it.

Radiative zone

Convective zone

Photosphere

This diagram shows the sun's layers. In reality, they are not so brightly colored, and the boundaries between them are not always so clearly defined.

Core

Chromosphere

Sunspots

The sun's surface is a busy place. Sunspots appear and fade away, patterns of granulation constantly change, and there are fluctuations in the light and energy emitted by the sun. Many of these changes are the result of something happening inside the sun that we cannot see. The challenge for scientists is to figure out what could be causing these changes.

Corona

Based on this principle, scientists have figured out the basic structure of the sun. At the center is the core, where the sun's energy is generated. Outside that is the radiative zone, where energy from the core is carried outward into the convective zone. Then comes the photosphere, where the energy takes the form of visible light. Above that are the chromosphere, corona, and heliosphere.

VIRTUAL SUN

Many scientists create computer models of the sun to test theories about how it works. First, they make sure that their virtual sun obeys the known laws of physics. Then they make a computer model that recreates a process they believe happens inside the sun. The computer shows what the effects on the sun's visible surface would be. If these match up with actual observations of the sun, the theory may be right.

13

Inside a Star

Unlike Earth, the sun is not solid. Instead, it is completely made up of gas and a state of matter called plasma. The density and temperature of the gas and plasma change as you move through the inside of the sun, and this how we separate the different layers. At the center of the sun is the core, which is the densest part. The force of gravity causes all the other layers press down on it, which is why it is so dense—about twenty times denser an iron. The core is also incredibly hot—27,000,000 degrees Fahrenheit 5,000,000 degrees Celsius)!

radiative zone (also called the radiation zone) is located outside the core. ere, energy generated by the core is moved toward the outer layers of the through a process called radiation. There are three ways to transfer heat energy from one place to another. In conduction and convection, energy ansferred between particles in a solid, liquid, or gas. Radiation, on the er hand, does not require contact between the heat source and the heated ct. This is why we feel the sun's heat, even though we are not touching it.

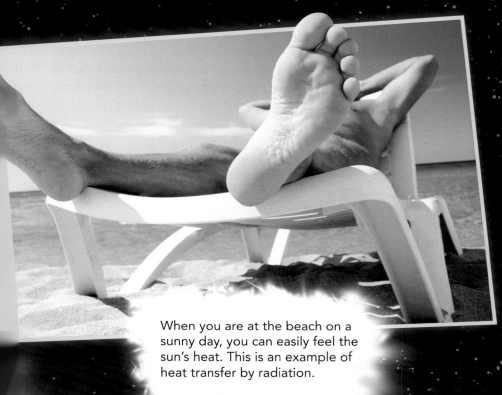

When you are at the beach on a sunny day, you can easily feel the sun's heat. This is an example of heat transfer by radiation.

One way that scientists study the interior of the sun is through a technique called helioseismology. The motion of the matter in the sun's outer layers produces sound waves. The waves are usually trapped inside the sun and bounce back and forth between its different parts. Scientists can study the way they bounce to learn about the temperature, density, and movement inside the sun.

Plasma is not just found in stars. Lightning is an example of plasma found on Earth.

WHAT IS PLASMA?

You probably know that all matter can exist in one of three states: solid, liquid, or gas. However, there is also a fourth state of matter. Plasma is similar to gas, but the atoms are different. Most atoms have a nucleus with electrons whizzing around it. In a plasma, the electrons are not bound to the nucleus, so they can move freely around the system. Gases can become plasmas when energy is added.

Moving Upward

Once energy travels out of the radiative zone, it moves into a cooler area called the convective zone. Where the core meets the radiative zone, the temperature decreases to about 12,500,000 degrees Fahrenheit (6,944,000 degrees C). By the time energy reaches the convective zone, it cools to about 3,600,000 degrees Fahrenheit (2,000,000 degrees C). As a result of this lower temperature, energy cannot travel as efficiently by radiation. Instead, it moves outward in a process known as convection.

Convection is what happens when a pan of water is put on the stove to boil. When the particles in the liquid are heated, they move faster and take up more space. This makes the hot areas of the liquid less dense than the cold areas. The hot liquid rises and the denser cold liquid moves to take its place. Eventually, this movement of hot and cold liquids heats everything in the pan. The same thing happens to gases in the convective zone of the sun.

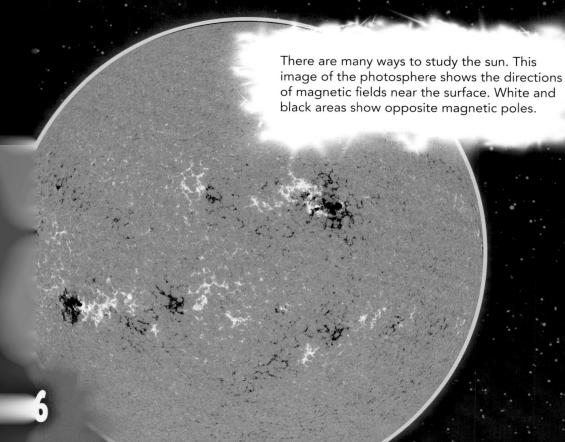

There are many ways to study the sun. This image of the photosphere shows the directions of magnetic fields near the surface. White and black areas show opposite magnetic poles.

Although the sun is not solid, in the inner layers the gas is so dense that we cannot see through it. Above the convection zone, however, is the photosphere, which is the first layer that we can study with telescopes and other tools. When looking at the photosphere we can see a pattern called granulation. This is caused by bubbles of hot and cool matter in the convection zone below. Although it is fairly cool in the photosphere—about 10,000 degrees Fahrenheit (5,538 degrees C), the gas is thin enough for radiation to take place again. Most of the heat and light that we receive on Earth was released by the photosphere.

FAST AND SLOW

In the radiative zone, energy from the sun's core is transferred from place to place by radiation. However, radiation does not just move in a single direction. The energy is passed randomly, sometimes moving outward, and other times moving inward or side-to-side. It can take more than 170,000 years for energy to get out of the radiation zone! It moves much more quickly through the convection zone, and can get to the top in a little over a week.

This pattern, seen on the surface of the sun, is called granulation. It is caused by thermal columns in the convective zone.

Why Does the Sun Shine?

The energy that reaches us on Earth has had a very long journey through the sun's layers, followed by a much shorter one (about eight minutes) through space. Where did it come from in the first place? The answer lies in a process called nuclear fusion, where atoms are ripped apart and put back together to form new substances.

In the sun's core, the temperature and pressure are high enough to destroy the internal structure of atoms. Most atoms are made up of a nucleus containing protons and neutrons, with electrons surrounding them. The sun is mainly made up of hydrogen atoms, which have one proton and one electron. When they interact with each other under extreme pressure, two nuclei can fuse, creating atoms of helium, which each have two protons in the nucleus. It takes several intermediate steps, but the helium atoms at the end have less mass than the two hydrogen atoms that started the process. The difference in mass is converted to energy, which then starts its journey out of the sun.

●	Proton
○	Neutron
○	Positron
●	Neutrino
γ	Gamma ray

The energy released during nuclear fusion takes the form of gamma rays, which then begin their journey outward through the sun's layers.

For a long time, scientists did not know how the sun created energy. New Zealand-born Ernest Rutherford (1871–1937) thought it might be caused by radioactive decay. It was a British physicist, Arthur Eddington (1882–1944), who first suggested in the 1920s that the temperature and pressure inside the sun could produce nuclear fusion. He drew on Albert Einstein's important theory about the relation between mass and energy. Scientists' observations of the sun since then have supported Eddington's theory.

A tokamak is a device that uses a magnetic field to confine plasma. The tokamak is used in experiments to try to create nuclear fusion.

FUSION ON EARTH

Scientists have been trying to create nuclear fusion in laboratories, because it is a potential source of clean energy that could eventually replace fossil fuels, such as oil and natural gas. However, we cannot recreate all the conditions that allow fusion in the sun's core. We can heat the plasma to incredibly high temperatures, but must use strong magnetic fields to contain it. So far, the energy required to produce fusion on Earth has nearly always been higher than the energy it generates.

19

Sunspots

From time to time, dark spots appear on the sun's visible surface: the photosphere. These are called sunspots, and they have been observed for many years. For example, Chinese astronomers recorded sunspots more than two thousand years ago. However, it took a long time for these spots to be understood. Most people who saw sunspots assumed they were objects passing in front of the sun. The Catholic Church's teachings at the time stated that the sun was perfect and unchanging—it would have seemed impossible that it could have had blemishes on its surface.

Eventually, most scientists accepted Galileo's theory that sunspots were actually on the surface of the sun, but they still did not know what caused them. In 1848, the U.S. scientist Joseph Henry (1797–1878) showed that sunspots were cooler than the surrounding areas. It was not until the twentieth century that astronomers realized that sunspots were caused by magnetic activity.

Galileo began studying sunspots in 1612. His theories about them eventually got him into trouble with the Catholic Church.

NOT-SO-HOT SPOTS

The average temperature of the photosphere is about 10,000 degrees Fahrenheit (5,538 degrees C) but sunspots are only about 6,000 degrees Fahrenheit (3,316 degrees C). For the sun, that is quite cool but it is still hot enough to boil iron! The darkest part of a sunspot, at the center, is called the umbra (the Greek word for shadow). The lighter region that surrounds it is called the penumbra.

Sunspots can appear singly or in clumps. This photograph shows a new sunspot colliding with an existing one, which resulted in a solar flare.

Deep inside the sun, magnetic fields are constantly being generated. As they rise through the sun's layers, they can bend or twist. Measurements of the sun's magnetism have shown that sunspots are areas of concentrated magnetic fields. Scientists used a tool called a spectroheliograph to detect magnetic fields on the sun.

One thing about sunspots that has been known for centuries is that they come and go. A sunspot can appear for as little as an hour or two, though some last for several months. Sometimes very few sunspots can be seen; at other times there are many more. Over the centuries astronomers have made detailed records of sunspots, and we now know that the number of sunspots rises and falls over an eleven-year cycle.

Chapter Three

ATMOSPHERE AND MAGNETISM

Just like Earth, the sun also has its own atmosphere. Although there is no solid boundary, the layers above the photosphere are usually known as the "solar atmosphere." They include the chromosphere and the corona. They are one of the easier regions of the sun to study because they can be viewed with many different types of telescopes.

The chromosphere is a layer of gas that is about 1,250 miles (two thousand kilometers) thick. It is much less dense than the photosphere, and without special equipment, it cannot normally be seen because the brightness of the photosphere drowns it out. In the chromosphere, energy is emitted as red light. Scientists can get a good look at the chromosphere by filtering out all other wavelengths of light, which leaves only the red light from the chromosphere.

Within the chromosphere, the temperature can rise to about 36,000 degrees Fahrenheit (20,000 degrees C). Above the chromosphere is a thin transition zone between the chromosphere and the corona, where the temperature rises even more, to about 1,800,000 degrees Fahrenheit (1,000,000 degrees C). The corona is the sun's outermost layer, and is very thin and faint. It can be seen from Earth only during a solar eclipse or by using a special telescope.

Scientists can use radio waves, gamma rays, and x-rays to study the sun's outer layers. Even so, there are still mysteries. For example, they are still not sure why the temperature is so high in these regions that are an incredibly far way from the heat-producing core. Astronomers are researching theories that might link the sun's magnetic field to the temperature rise.

During a total solar eclipse, the moon blocks out the bright light of the photosphere, allowing us to see the fainter light of the corona.

A LAYER OF SPIKES

The chromosphere appears to have a jagged, constantly changing outer layer. This is caused by long, thin "fingers" of glowing gas that rise from the bottom. They are called spicules. It takes them about ten to fifteen minutes to rise to the top of the chromosphere, traveling at a speed of twelve miles per second (19 km per second), and then sink back down again. Gas from the chromosphere also forms prominences, which are large loops that rise thirty thousand miles (48,280 km) from the sun's surface.

23

Solar Wind

The sun's hot corona is the source of a phenomenon known as the solar wind. This is a stream of charged particles that flows out in all directions, extending far beyond Neptune. The area where the solar wind blows is called the heliosphere, and it is like a huge bubble, embedded within the ambient gas, dust, and magnetic fields of the galaxy.

The particles of the solar wind can escape the sun's gravity because the high temperature of the corona gives them a lot of energy. They travel extremely fast: anywhere between 670,000 and 1.8 million miles per hour (1,080,000 and 1,120,000 km per hour). The speed of the solar wind changes a lot, and in places high-speed wind can catch up with low-speed wind.

UP CLOSE AND PERSONAL

In 1997, the National Aeronautics and Space Administration (NASA) launched the Advanced Composition Explorer (ACE) spacecraft to study several topics, including the solar wind. It orbits in a position where the force of Earth's gravity and the sun's are about equal, approximately one million miles (1,600,000 km) from Earth. It has a variety of tools for monitoring the solar wind, and it provides data that helps forecast solar storms.

When a geomagnetic storm is on the way, the ACE spacecraft can give us about one hour's advance warning.

Earth has an invisible magnetic field surrounding it, which protects us from some types of solar radiation. When the solar wind hits Earth's magnetic field, most of it is deflected and travels around the planet instead of reaching the surface. However, the solar wind still has an effect. Sometimes when it interacts with the magnetic field, it causes the auroras, better known as the Northern and Southern Lights. It also occasionally causes geomagnetic storms, which can disrupt satellites and electronic devices.

We are lucky to have our magnetic field to protect us. Planets with no magnetic fields (or very weak ones) can have their atmosphere stripped away by the force of the solar wind. For example, Mars's weak magnetic field is not strong enough to provide much protection, and the solar wind has stripped away much of the atmosphere that it once had.

The Northern Lights are a breathtaking sight, illuminating the sky with eerie, shimmering light.

Solar Flares and Coronal Mass Ejections

Seen from Earth, the sun appears constant and unchanging, but the sun's surface and atmosphere are regions of sometimes violent activity. One example of this is a solar flare: an enormous explosion that takes place on the surface of the sun. During a solar flare, sections of the sun's matter are heated to millions of degrees in just a few minutes, releasing huge amounts of energy. The energy can take the form of gamma rays, x-rays, and charged particles.

For many years astronomers thought that solar flares were the main type of explosion on the sun. In the 1970s however, scientists found evidence of the existence of a much bigger type of explosion: the coronal mass ejection (CME). A CME occurs when a solar prominence erupts and sends a large amount of matter out into the solar system. When a CME collides with Earth's magnetosphere, it can shut down electricity grids, as well as interfering with radio communications and damaging satellites.

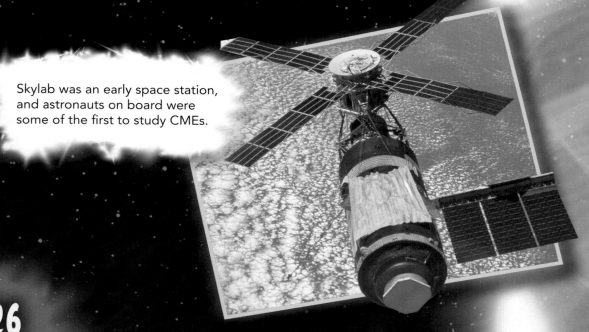

Skylab was an early space station, and astronauts on board were some of the first to study CMEs.

This image was taken using a coronagraph to block out the bright light of the photosphere. You can see the loop of a CME near the top.

This dramatic image of a CME bursting out from the sun was taken by NASA's Solar Dynamics Observatory (SDO).

MAKE THE CONNECTION

Both solar flares and CMEs are related to the same magnetic activity that causes sunspots. For example, solar flares usually occur near sunspots. Solar flares and CMEs also follow the eleven-year solar cycle. At the solar minimum, when there are few sunspots, there is about one CME per week. At the solar maximum, when sunspots are at their peak, there are two or three CMEs per day.

It took so long to discover CMEs because the corona is difficult to observe from Earth. Normally, it is visible only during a total solar eclipse, and these events are rare. Astronomers can study the corona at other times by using a coronagraph, which creates an artificial eclipse by blocking out the bright disc of the sun. However, coronagraphs on ground-based telescopes show only the innermost part of the corona; the rest is drowned out by the brightness of the sky. From space you can see more of the corona, so orbiting spacecraft are crucial for studying this volatile region.

Chapter Four

BIRTH AND DEATH OF THE SUN

Stars are not living things, but the terms used to describe them often make it sound as though they were. We use terms such as "birth," "life," and "death," but these are not meant literally—they are just a way of making difficult concepts more understandable. Stars are even described as having a "life cycle," which means that over the course of many years, they are formed, they change, and eventually, they stop shining.

The sun is just one of trillions of stars in the universe, and it is following the same series of stages as all other stars. It began in a giant cloud of gas and dust called a nebula. A nebula can have enough raw material to make thousands of stars. Inside the nebula, the gas and dust starts to clump together. Eventually these growing clumps form protostars, which start to heat up.

This nebula is about 5,500 light years away from Earth. Its clouds of gas and dust will eventually form new stars.

Brown dwarfs are "failed stars." They form in the same way as stars, but never ignite. They are hard to find because they are so dim.

CLOSE, BUT NO STAR

If a protostar is not massive enough for nuclear fusion, it will never begin to shine. It will become what is known as a brown dwarf, and over the next few billion years, it will slowly cool down. The smallest brown dwarfs are only about twice the mass of Jupiter. These "failed stars" were just a theory until they were actually discovered in 1995. Now some astronomers think that there might be as many brown dwarfs in the universe as there are stars.

What happens next depends on how big the protostar is. It must have a certain amount of mass in order to create temperatures high enough for nuclear fusion to start. If the protostar has enough mass—approximately 8 percent of the mass of our sun or more—then the core will heat up to millions of degrees Fahrenheit. The process of nuclear fusion will start, and the star will begin to shine. Once this happens, the star is called a "main sequence star," and it will remain this way until its fuel begins to run out. About 90 percent of the stars in the universe, including our sun, are main sequence stars.

Red Giant

Stars do not live forever. The nuclear fusion taking place in their cores presses outward, balancing the force of gravity pulling inward. This makes the star stable, but eventually the fuel will run out, and the star will "die." How long this takes depends on how big the star is. A really massive star has a lot of fuel, but it also has stronger gravity, which makes the core hotter. This means that the star will burn through its fuel a lot faster than a smaller star would.

GOING OUT WITH A BANG

If the sun were a lot larger than it is, it would not eventually turn into a red giant. Instead, it would burn through its fuel much more quickly and end up with a helium core, which would fuse into heavier and heavier elements, surrounded by a huge shell of cooling, expanding gas. Eventually the element iron would form in the core and further nuclear fusion would cease. At this point, the gravity of the core would cause it to collapse under its own weight and blow itself apart in a massive explosion called a supernova.

This cloud is all that remains of a massive star after a supernova. The image was made using data from three different space telescopes, each detecting a different kind of energy.

When the sun turns into a red giant, Earth will be nothing more than a barren, dry planet, illuminated by an enormous reddish-orange sun.

Our sun, which is a medium-sized star, will exist as a main sequence star for about ten billion years. However, a star about ten times as massive as the sun will last for only about twenty million years. At the other end of the spectrum, a star with half the mass of the sun can probably last for eighty to one hundred billion years, which is much longer than the universe has existed.

The sun formed about 4.6 billion years ago so it is nearly halfway through its life. In billions of years, when its fuel starts to run out, the core will begin to contract and get hotter. The outer layers of the sun will expand, becoming so big that they extend past the current orbit of Mars. Earth would be swallowed up, its oceans evaporated and its atmosphere stripped away. At that point the sun would be known as a red giant. Eventually the outer layers will drift away, leaving the dying core to cool and dim, becoming a white dwarf. When the core stops shining altogether it is called a black dwarf.

The Solar Cycle

In addition to its life cycle, the sun goes through another, much shorter cycle called the solar cycle. Approximately every eleven years, the sun reaches a peak of magnetic activity. This peak is called the solar maximum and during this time there are visible sunspots nearly all the time. At the opposite end of the cycle, the solar minimum, sunspots are rare and only last a short time.

Other types of solar activity, such as solar flares and CMEs, are also caused by the sun's magnetism. They also follow the solar cycle and are much more common around the solar maximum. However, you have probably never noticed the changes in the sun's output. Over the course of a solar cycle, the maximum change in the sun's radiation is fewer than 0.1 percent of its total output.

Even though humans do not notice the sun being any hotter or brighter during the solar maximum, there are still effects felt on Earth. For example, during these periods there are more solar flares and CMEs. These can send radiation toward Earth that damages satellites and spacecraft and can disrupt electronic communications.

However, the detailed records of sunspots we have, which go back centuries, show that the sun's output can affect Earth's climate over long periods. Between 1645 and 1714 there were almost no sunspots, and this coincides with the peak of the "Little Ice Age," an unusually cool period that affected Europe from the 1300s to the 1800s.

RINGS OF EVIDENCE?

One interesting phenomenon is that tree rings seem to show evidence of sunspot activity. If you slice through a tree's trunk, you will see a growth ring corresponding to each year of its life. During a year when conditions are good, a tree will grow more, resulting in a thick ring. In a bad year, for example, during a drought, the ring will be thinner. Some evidence shows that tree rings seem to follow an eleven-year cycle, corresponding to the solar cycle, but scientists are not yet sure exactly why this is.

During the solar maximum, there can be as many as one hundred visible sunspots at any given time.

Chapter Five

ECLIPSES

While Earth travels around the sun, the moon is traveling around Earth. Once a month, the moon passes between Earth and the sun. If they are aligned just right, the moon will block the sun's light, causing a shadow to fall on part of Earth. This is called an eclipse. During a total solar eclipse, the sky slowly dims until it becomes dark, and the temperature drops. For people thousands of years ago, who did not understand how it happened, eclipses could be terrifying.

Not all eclipses completely block out the sun, though. There are four types of solar eclipses: total, partial, annular, and hybrid. In a total eclipse, everything lines up perfectly and the moon completely blocks out the sun. In a partial eclipse, the moon and the sun do not quite line up, so the moon only partially covers the disc of the sun, leaving a crescent shape.

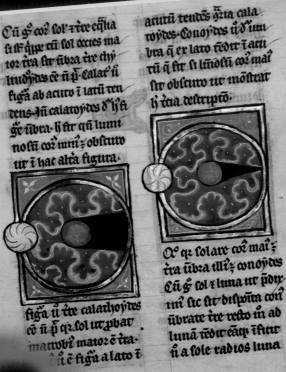

Sometimes the moon is slightly farther away from Earth than at other times, making it appear smaller in the sky. This can lead to an annular eclipse, when a bright ring is visible around the moon. A hybrid eclipse appears as a total eclipse from some parts of Earth's surface and as an annular eclipse from other regions before becoming a total eclipse.

Astronomers have understood eclipses for a long time. This book from the thirteenth century includes diagrams showing how the moon blocks the sun.

In this annular eclipse, the moon did not appear large enough in the sky to completely block out the sun.

JUST RIGHT

Earth is a great place for viewing solar eclipses. Someone living on Mercury or Venus would never see an eclipse because these planets have no moons to block the sun. Mars's moons are too small to cause a total eclipse. The sun is about four hundred times bigger in diameter than our moon, but it is also about four hundred times farther away. This means that the sun and moon appear almost exactly the same size in the sky, causing amazing total eclipses.

The moon does not orbit exactly in line with Earth's orbit around the sun. If it did, we would have a solar eclipse every month. The moon's orbit is slightly tilted, so we get eclipses only when the two paths intersect. In most years there are only a few solar eclipses, and each one is only visible from a relatively small area of Earth's surface.

Phases of an Eclipse

Total solar eclipses are one of the most amazing phenomena seen on Earth, but they are rare. They happen about once every eighteen months, but can be seen only from a specific location (such as a specific town). During a total eclipse, the moon's shadow follows a path about ten thousand miles (16,000 km) long but only one hundred miles (161 km) wide. Only people within that area will see the sun become completely covered.

During a total solar eclipse, the first thing visible from Earth will be a tiny bite out of the side of the sun. This is called "first contact." Over the next hour and a half or so, the moon covers more and more of the sun, and when there is only a small crescent left, this is "second contact." The light on Earth is dimmer at that point. A few minutes before totality, the crescent is reduced to a few tiny specks of light around the edge, called Baily's Beads. When only one bright "bead" is left, the sun looks like a diamond ring.

After first contact, the moon's shadow starts to cover more and more of the sun. In a partial eclipse, only part of it ever gets covered.

The "diamond ring effect" gets its name because the visible part of the sun looks like a ring with a large diamond.

STAY SAFE

It is never safe to look directly at the sun, except for during the few moments of totality. Even when 99 percent of the sun's surface is obscured, the remaining part is still bright enough to damage your eyes. Sunglasses are not enough to protect your eyes; you need a specially-made filter to watch a solar eclipse. The safest way of viewing an eclipse is by making a pinhole in a piece of cardboard, and letting the sun shine through that hole onto a white piece of paper, where you will see a projected image of the sun.

During totality the sun's corona shines around the disc of the moon. Totality lasts for only a few minutes, and then the eclipse reaches "third contact" when the photosphere starts to emerge from behind the sun. The diamond ring effect may be visible again before the moon moves farther away. "Fourth contact" occurs when the full disc of the sun is seen again.

Studying the Corona

total solar eclipse offers a rare chance to study the sun's corona. In fact, it is the only time that the corona is visible from arth with the naked eye. Amateur observers can also see other ings during a total eclipse. For example, in the first few seconds totality, a red streak is often visible along the side of the moon. his is the reddish light of the chromosphere, which normally annot be seen because of the brightness of the photosphere.

though the corona is not visible from Earth at other times, acecraft such as the SDO or the Solar and Heliospheric oservatory (SOHO) can see it at all times. However, the ronagraphs that they use block out the innermost section the corona, so scientists make use of solar eclipses to get good view of this part. Another good reason for studying e corona from Earth during eclipses is that it is much cheaper d more flexible to send a team of scientists to view an lipse than it is to launch a spacecraft!

ring a solar eclipse, astronomers can measure the temperature the corona by using spectroscopy. They can also look for rations in the corona that might give a clue as to the reason its incredibly high temperatures. Advances in technology mean t computer images are now able to bring out low-contrast features that had not been seen in previous eclipses.

Astronauts on the International Space Station (ISS) took this photograph of the path of the moon's shadow during a solar eclipse in 2006. Areas of Earth not in the shadow would not have seen the eclipse at all.

HISTORICAL DISCOVERIES

In the days before spacecraft, eclipses were the only way to study the corona, and it was during an eclipse that helium was discovered. In 1868, while observing an eclipse in India, Pierre Janssen (1824–1907) used a spectrograph and found a bright yellow line in a solar prominence. It was caused by an undiscovered element, which was called helium. Helium was not found on Earth until 1895. In 1930, an eclipse gave a German astronomer the evidence he needed to estimate the temperature of the corona.

Park rangers at Arches National Park in Utah helped visitors safely view an annular solar eclipse in 2012.

39

Chapter Six

WHAT'S NEXT?

At any given time there are several different spacecraft studying the sun. Each has its own goals, along with tools specially designed to get the data they need. Here are just a few of them.

ACE: This NASA probe studies particles coming both from the sun and from interstellar sources. It measures and compares the composition of the corona, solar wind, and other types of matter.

Hinode: This probe was launched by the Japanese Aerospace Exploration Agency (JAXA) with collaboration from NASA and the United Kingdom. It has an optical telescope that observes solar magnetic fields, as well as an x-ray telescope and a ultraviolet (UV) imaging spectrometer for studying the corona. It was designed to learn more about the heating of the corona, as well as the causes of solar flares and the sun's magnetic fields.

SOHO: This incredibly successful joint project between NASA and the European Space Agency (ESA) studied the sun from its core to the outer corona. Its main goals were to use helioseismology to explore the structure of the sun, investigate coronal heating, and find out how the solar wind is produced.

Hinode captured this amazing image of a transit of Venus in 2012. You can see the dark shape of Venus moving across the surface of the sun.

On September 24, 2013, the SOHO spacecraft watched as a prominence on the sun became unmistakable and finally blew out into space.

Picard: This French probe takes detailed measurements of the sun's diameter and shape to see how these features are linked to solar activity.

STEREO: This mission is actually made up of two spacecraft that work together to produce 3D images of CMEs. Another of its objectives is to trace the flow of energy and matter from the sun to Earth.

FINDING THE BEST SPOT

The spacecraft studying the sun follow different orbits, depending on what they are observing. Hinode travels around Earth's poles, passing over the same part of Earth at roughly the same time each day, so that it can look at sun at all times. Other spacecraft orbit the sun at the point where the sun's gravity and Earth's own gravity balance each other out. The Solar Terrestrial Relations Observatory (STEREO) spacecraft more or less follow Earth's orbit, but one travels ahead of Earth and the other one is behind.

41

Solar Dynamics Observatory

The sun has a huge effect on life on Earth, and understanding how this works is extremely important. Several space probes, among them Cluster-II, Geotail, THEMIS, and TIMED, have been launched to study Earth's atmosphere and magnetosphere in detail. Such probes help scientists learn more about how the sun influences weather and other conditions on Earth.

The energy given off by the sun is variable, meaning that it produces different amounts and types of energy at different times. When experienced on Earth, this variability is known as "space weather." SDO, launched by NASA in 2010, was designed to study the sun from the inside out in order to learn more about the processes inside the sun that create this space weather. Once scientists have a better understanding of how space weather is created, they will be better able to predict it.

SDO has an imaging tool that uses helioseismology to "see" beneath the sun's surface. The processes that create the sun's magnetic field begin deep within its interior, and scientists hope that the tool will help them understand how the fields are created. The imager is also able to map magnetic fields. SDO also has four different telescopes for observing the sun's surface and atmosphere. The telescopes have different filters, which allow them to view the sun in ten different wavelengths of light.

SDO's tools turn different wavelengths of light into an image that we can see. This composite shows images of the sun taken at different wavelengths, each shown in a different color.

SDO captured this image of
a mid-level solar flare in 2014,
using a tool that detects UV light.

LIVING WITH A STAR

SDO is part of NASA's "Living With a Star" program, which focuses on studying the aspects of the sun that most directly affect life on Earth. For example, the goal of SDO is to learn how solar activity is created, and how this activity creates space weather. Other space probes in this program include the Van Allen Probes, which study the radiation belts that surround Earth.

Another tool in the SDO's arsenal is the Extreme Ultraviolet Variability Experiment (EVE). This measures fluctuations in the sun's UV output, which heats Earth's upper atmosphere. These fluctuations have an effect on satellites (including GPS satellites) and communications systems, so predicting them is a key goal.

Looking to the Future

Although scientists have made many incredible discoveries about the sun, there is still a lot to learn and many mysteries to be solved. One of the biggest mysteries is why the corona is so hot, and scientists are also trying to discover the precise causes of solar flares and CMEs. Once they figure this out, they may be able to predict when and where they will take place, and how big they will be. A third big area of study is the cause of the solar cycle.

Astronomers hope that some of these questions will be answered by the Solar Orbiter, a joint project between NASA and ESA. It is designed to explore how the sun's heliosphere is created and controlled. To do this, it must travel closer to the sun than most other spacecraft do. Another NASA probe, Solar Probe+, will go even closer as it studies the outer corona. At its closest approach, it will travel only 3.67 million miles (5,900,000 km) from the sun's photosphere. In order to survive the harsh conditions found there, the spacecraft has a solar shadow shield made of a reinforced carbon composite material.

The Indian Space Research Organisation (ISRO) celebrated a first for the country when its Mars probe entered orbit around the planet in 2014. Building on that success, its Aditya probe is designed to study the sun's corona, with a focus on CMEs.

Astronauts on their way to the ISS depend on spacecraft studying the sun to predict solar weather and radiation that may affect their safety.

Humans have always been fascinated by the sun. Now, with advanced technology, we are able to learn more about it than ever before. Perhaps the students of today will be the ones to solve more of the sun's mysteries in the future!

This illustration of Solar Probe+ near the sun shows the shadow shield that will protect its components from the sun's energy.

MISSING NEUTRINOS

Every atom is made up of smaller particles, such as protons and electrons, which are called subatomic particles. Neutrinos are a type of subatomic particle that can pass easily through normal matter. They are released by the reactions in the sun's core and travel straight out through the sun and into space. Some of them should reach Earth, but so far scientists have only been able to detect about one-third as many neutrinos as they would expect. They are working hard to solve the mystery of the missing neutrinos.

GLOSSARY

atoms The smallest possible units of chemical elements.

chromosphere The layer of gas that surrounds the sun above the photosphere and below the corona.

conduction A way of transferring heat between substances that are in direct contact with each other.

convection A way of transferring heat in a liquid or gas; when warmer, less dense material moves upward and is replaced by cooler, denser material.

convective zone The area of the sun that is outside the radiative zone but just below the photosphere.

corona The outer atmosphere of the sun.

coronal mass ejection (CME) A massive burst of solar energy released into space.

ecliptic The apparent path of the sun, as seen from Earth against the background stars.

electromagnetic radiation A kind of radiation including visible light, radio waves, gamma waves, and x-rays.

electrons Tiny particles with a negative charge that moves outside the nucleus of an atom.

equinoxes The two times during the year when day and night are both twelve hours long all over the world.

helioseismology The technique of measuring sound waves as they travel through the sun in order to learn about its internal structure.

heliosphere The area of space in which the solar wind is felt.

infrared radiation A type of electromagnetic energy with a long wavelength, which cannot be seen as visible light.

magnetic fields The spaces around magnets in which magnetic forces are active.

magnetosphere The region surrounding a planet or other object in which its magnetic field is the dominant magnetic field.

mass A measure of how much matter is in an object.

nuclear fusion The chemical process in which the nuclei of two or more atoms fuse into a more massive nucleus. This process releases a huge amount of energy.

nucleus The center of something, such as an atom.

orbit The curved path that one body in space takes around another, such as a moon orbiting a planet.

photosphere The bright visible surface of the sun.

plasma A state of matter in which electrons float free of their nucleus, forming an ionized gas.

radiation Waves of energy sent out by sources of heat or light, such as the sun.

radiative zone The area of the sun just outside the core, below the convective zone.

solar wind A flow of charged particles that travels from the sun into the solar system.

solstices The days of the year with either the shortest period of daylight (the winter solstice) or the shortest period of darkness (the summer solstice).

spectroscopy The technique of observing light from an object to find out its composition, temperature, speed, or density.

sunspots The dark patches that are sometimes seen on the surface of the sun.

transit When a planet or other object passes directly between Earth and the sun so that it can be seen from Earth as it moves across the disc of the sun.

FOR MORE INFORMATION

Books

Aguilar, David A. *Space Encyclopedia: A Tour of Our Solar System and Beyond.* Washington, D.C.: National Geographic Kids, 2013.

Farndon, John. *What Do We Know About Stars and Galaxies?* (Earth, Space, & Beyond). Chicago, IL: Heinemann-Raintree, 2011.

Hunter, Nick. *Stars and Galaxies* (Astronaut Travel Guides). Chicago, IL: Heinemann-Raintree, 2012.

Simon, Seymour. *Our Solar System.* New York, NY: HarperCollins, 2014.

Sparrow, Giles. *Destination the Sun* (Destination Solar System). New York, NY: PowerKids Press, 2009.

Taylor-Butler, Christine. *The Sun* (True Books: Space). Danbury, CT: Children's Press, 2014.

Websites

Due to the changing nature of Internet links, Rosen Publishing has developed an online list of websites related to the subject of this book. This site is updated regularly. Please use this link to access the list:

http://www.rosenlinks.com/SSS/Sun

INDEX